CW00548489

Introduction to Patents and Patent Law in India

Siva Prasad Bose and Joy Bose

Published by Joy Bose, 2022.

Introduction to Patents and Patent Law in India

By Siva Prasad Bose and Joy Bose

Published by Joy Bose

INTRODUCTION TO PATENTS AND PATENT LAW IN INDIA

First edition. February 23, 2022.

Copyright © 2022 Siva Prasad Bose and Joy Bose.

ISBN: 979-8201002039

Written by Siva Prasad Bose and Joy Bose.

Table of Contents

Dedication

———

This book is dedicated to all patent inventors in India, whose ideas can play a big role in turning India into a leader in the field of innovation.

Contents

─────

Preface

———

Patents are a key component of intellectual property and vital to the process of innovation. They serve multiple uses. One is to reward inventors and motivate them to create inventing for the betterment of society, inculcating a culture of innovation. Another is to protect inventors from getting their ideas stolen and profited from by unscrupulous people.

In this book we introduce the laws related to patents and Intellectual property in India. We discuss the patent filing process in India, and other aspects of filing and persecution of patents. We also discuss the steps that are to be taken for ideation, and how to make a better patent, from the point of view of patent inventors.

Chapter 1: Introduction to Patent Laws in India

———

Patents along with trademarks and copyright come under Intellectual property or IP. In this chapter we give an overview of the Intellectual Property (IP) law in India, what are the types of intellectual property and what is covered under the patent law.

1.1 What is intellectual property (IP)

Intellectual property refers to creations and new ideas originating in the human mind, rather than in a tangible form such as other forms of property. They include copyrights, trademarks, patents and industrial designs. The law treats them as property in the sense that the owners or inventors of them have the legal rights to profit from them and transfer or license them to others if they so wish. The TRIPS agreement of World Trade Organization or WTO governs rules related to patents and other IPs across countries.

1.1.1 Patents

Patent are granted for inventions of a product or process for manufacturing a product. They give rights to the inventors of the product to prevent them from being copied by others. These are governed by the Patents Act 1970 in India. Patent Cooperation Treaty or PCT of 1970 governs patents around the world, and patents can be filed in multiple countries together using the

World Intellectual Property Organization or WIPO under the provisions of the PCT.

1.1.2 Industrial designs

These cover the visual design of the product, including its look and feel. It can include characteristics like shape and color of the product. Examples include design of a chip. Designs Act of 2000 is the law in India that governs industrial designs.

1.1.3 Geographical indicators

These refer to products that refer to a country or place where the product is associated with as been manufactured. An example is Alphonso mango or Banarasi sarees. The law for them is defined in the Geographical Indications of Goods Act of 1999.

1.1.4 Copyrights

Copyright refers to created works including books, as well as artistic works such as songs and paintings. The laws around copyrights are intended to prevent the created works from being copied, and ensure that the original creator alone gets to profit from their created work. The Copyrights Act 1957 governs these.

1.1.5 Trademarks

Trademarks are granted for unique visual symbols or indicators of a manufacturer or vendors of products, such as logo of a company. They are registered under the trade-mark registry. The aim of trademarks is to make sure the product is not copied and is an indicator of the quality and brand of the product, so the customers and other stakeholders can identify it when deciding the buy the product. Trademarks Act of 1999 governs the law in India related to trademarks.

1.2 What is the Patent law in India

As mentioned, various kinds of intellectual property have their own laws in India, that together comprise the IP regime. The laws include the Copyright Act 1957 (governing copyrights), Patents Act 1970, Trademarks Act 1999, Designs Act 2000 (covering industrial designs) and so on.

In this book we focus on the laws related to patents.

Patent law in India is governed by the acts in the following subsections.

1.2.1 Patents Act 1970

This is the original act that consolidates the patent laws in India. This has been amended by the Patents Amendment Act of 2005.

Some of the important sections of the Patents Act 1970 are as follows:

Section 3 specifies what are not considered as inventions under the Act: (words of the act are in italics)

• *an invention which is frivolous or which claims anything obviously contrary to well established natural laws;*

• *an invention the primary or intended use or commercial exploitation of which could be contrary public order or morality or which causes serious prejudice to human, animal or plant life or health or to the environment;*

• *the mere discovery of a scientific principle or the formulation of an abstract theory or discovery of any living thing or non-living substance occurring in nature;*

• *the mere discovery of a new form of a known substance which does not result in the enhancement of the known efficacy of that substance or the mere discovery of any new property or new use for a known substance or of the mere use of a known process, machine or apparatus unless such known process results in a new product or employs at least one new reactant.*

• *Inventions related to atomic energy are not patentable*

Section 6 describes which persons are entitled to apply for patent:

• by any person claiming to be the true and first inventor of the invention;

• by any person being the assignee of the person claiming to be the true and first

• inventor in respect of the right to make such an application;

• by the legal representative of any deceased person who immediately before his death was entitled to make such an application.

Section 7 describes how the patent application which is filed in the patent office, in the prescribed forms and what is the filing date.

Section 9 describes what is a provisional specification and complete specification. If a patent has been filed as provisional, the complete specification should be filed within 12 months.

Section 10 describes the content of the specification. It should begin with a title, should be accompanied by drawings as needed, fully and particularly describe the invention and its method, disclose the best method for performing the invention, end with a list of claims of the inventions and accompanied by an abstract.

Section 11 describes the process of publication and of patent applications. Section 12 describes the process for examination of the application by the examiner. Section 13 describes to the prior art search for anticipation of the patent by previous publication. Sections 15 to 20 describe the powers of the controller with respect to date of the patent, being anticipated by earlier patents, potential infringement, substitution of the patent application etc.

THE PATENTS ACT, 1970
[39 of 1970, dt. 19-9-1970]
[As amended by Patents (Amdt.) Act, 2005 (15 of 2005), dt. 4-4-2005]

An Act to amend and consolidate the law relating to patents
Be it enacted by Parliament in the Twenty first Year of the Republic of India as follows:

CHAPTER I
PRELIMINARY

1. Short title, extent and commencement

(1) This Act may be called the Patents Act, 1970.

(2) It extends to the whole of India.

(3) It shall come into force on such date as the Central Government may, by notification in the Official Gazette, appoint:

PROVIDED that different dates may be appointed for different provisions of this Act, and any reference in any such provision to the commencement of this Act shall be construed as a reference to the coming into force of that provision.

2. Definitions and interpretation

(1) In this Act, unless the context otherwise requires,—

[(a) "Appellate Board" means the Appellate Board referred to in section 116;

(ab) "assignee" includes an assignee of the assignee and the legal representative of a deceased assignee and references to the assignee of any person include references to the assignee of the legal representative or assignee of that person;

[(aba) "Budapest Treaty" means the Budapest Treaty on the International Recognition of the Deposit of Micro-organisms for the Purposes of Patent Procedure done at Budapest on 28th day of April, 1977, as amended and modified from time to time;]

(ac) "capable of industrial application", in relation to an invention, means that the invention is capable of being made or used in an industry;]

(b) "Controller" means the Controller-General of Patents, Designs and Trade Marks referred to in section 73;

(c) "convention application" means an application for a patent made by virtue of section 135;

[(d) "convention country" means a country or a country which is member of a group of countries or a union of countries or an Inter-governmental organisation preferred to as a convention country in section 133;]]

(e) "district court" has the meaning assigned to that expression by the CPC, 1908;

(f) "exclusive licence" means a licence from a patentee which confers on the licensee, or on the licensee and persons authorised by him, to the exclusion of

Figure: The Patents Act 1970

Section 25 and onwards specifies the opposition proceedings, how someone can oppose the grant of a patent and on what grounds, such as the claim is after the priority date, or that the invention was publicly known or used in India before the claims, or that it is not an invention under the act, or that the patentee has not disclosed all relevant information, and so on.

Section 43 onwards describe the grant of patents and what are the rights of a patent awardee. Section 54 onwards describe patent of addition and amendments to a patent. Section 60 onwards describe issues such as restoration of lapsed patents, surrender and revocation of patents. Section 67 and later sections go through the register of patents, things related to the patent office and its branches, and powers of the controller. Section 82 discusses compulsory licenses, such as when the patent is an essential drug or essential to the well-being of society and is not widely available at a reasonable cost.

Section 104 onwards deal with suits for the infringement of patents, and the power of courts to grant relief for infringement. Here the burden of proof lies on the defendant.

Hence, the Patents Act 1970 is a very comprehensive act and covers different sections of patent filing, infringement and powers of the controller and the courts.

1.2.2 Patents (Amendment) Act 2005

This act modified the Indian patents act to be conforming with the Trade-Related Aspects of Intellectual Property Rights (TRIPS) agreement of the World Trade Organization (WTO).

Its provisions amend various sections of the original patents act 1970.

Some example sections of the Patents Amendment Act are as follows:

16. In section 17 of the principal Act, in sub-section (1), for the words "before acceptance of the complete specification", the words "before the grant of the patent" shall be substituted.

17. In section 18 of the principal Act,—

(a) in sub-section (1), for the words "to accept the complete specification", the words "the application" shall be substituted;

(b) sub-section (4) shall be omitted.

MINISTRY OF LAW AND JUSTICE

(Legislative Department)

New Delhi, the 5th April, 2005/Chaitra 15,1927 (Saka)

The following Act of Parliament received the assent of the President on 4th April, 2005, and is hereby published for general information:—

THE PATENTS (AMENDMENT) ACT, 2005

No. 15 OF 2005

[4th April, 2005.]

An Act further to amend the Patents Act, 1970.

BE it enacted by Parliament in the Fifty-sixth Year of the Republic of India as follows:—

1. (*1*) This Act may be called the Patents (Amendment) Act, 2005.

    (2) Sub-clause (*ii*) of clause (*a*), and clause (*b*), of section 37, sections 41,42,47,59 to 63 (both inclusive) and 74 shall come into force on such date as the Central Government may, by notification in the Official Gazette, appoint; and the remaining provisions of this Act shall be deemed to have come into force on the 1st day of January, 2005.

Short title and commencement.

39 of 1970

2. In section 2 of the Patents Act, 1970 (hereinafter referred to as the principal Act), in sub-section (*1*),—

Amendment of section 2.

    (a) after clause (*ab*), the following clause shall be inserted, namely:—

    '*(aba)* "Budapest Treaty" means the Budapest Treaty on the International Recognition of the Deposit of Micro-organisms for the Purposes of Patent Procedure done at Budapest on 28th day of April, 1977, as amended and modified from time to time;';

    (b) in clause (*d*), for the words, brackets and figures "notified as such under sub-section (*1*) of section 133", the words and figures "referred to as a convention country in section 133" shall be substituted;

    (c) clause (*g*) shall be omitted;

    (d) in clause (*h*),—

        (*i*) in sub-clause (*iii*), after the words and figures "the Companies Act, 1956", the word "; or" shall be inserted;

1 of 1956

        (*ii*) after sub-clause (*iii*), the following sub-clause shall be inserted, namely:—

        "*(iv)* by an institution wholly or substantially financed by the Government;";

        (*iii*) the words "and includes the Council of Scientific and Industrial Research and any other institution which is financed wholly or for the major part by the said Council;" shall be omitted;

    (e) for clause (*i*), the following clause shall be substituted, namely:—

    '*(i)* "High Court", in relation to a State or Union territory, means the High Court having territorial jurisdiction in that State or Union territory, as the case may be;';

    (f) for clause (*ja*), the following clause shall be substituted, namely:—

    '*(ja)* "inventive step" means a feature of an invention that involves technical advance as compared to the existing knowledge or having economic significance or both and that makes the invention not obvious to a person skilled in the art,';

Figure: The Patents (Amendment) Act 2005

1.2.3 The Patents (Amendment) Rules 2019

This contains detailed rules on e-filing of patents and similar procedures.

The Gazette of India

EXTRAORDINARY

भाग II—खण्ड 3—उप-खण्ड (i)
PART II—Section 3—Sub-section (i)

प्राधिकार से प्रकाशित
PUBLISHED BY AUTHORITY

सं. 540]   नई दिल्ली, मंगलवार, सितम्बर 17, 2019/भाद्र 26, 1941
No. 540]   NEW DELHI, TUESDAY, SEPTEMBER 17, 2019/BHADRA 26, 1941

Figure: The Patent Rules 2019

These rules include special provisions for small companies and startups, for women and some categories that qualify for expedited examination of the patent applications. They also discuss changes to a few previous rules that were applicable.

1.3 Offices dealing with Patents

The Indian Patent Office or IPO is the main organization that deals with patents in India. Its head office is in Kolkata and it has branches in Chennai, New Delhi and Mumbai. The website is https://ipindia.gov.in/.

Each of these offices covers a number of states in India. For example, patents from Bangalore, Karnataka organizations would be filed with the Chennai office, that covers South India. Patents from West Bengal and Orissa would be covered by the office in Kolkata while those from UP and North India by the Delhi office.

The Indian Patent Office comes under the Office of the Controller General of Patents, Designs & Trade Marks (CGPDTM) which deals with all IP related areas. Its office is located in Mumbai.

1.4 Patent Agents and Patent Attorneys

Patent attorneys are lawyers who are well versed in patent law and can file and fight court cases related to patent infringement. They have law degrees and have passed the bar exam and are registered with the state bar council.

Patent Agents are those professional people who are skilled in patent drafting and patent filing and related areas, who have qualified and passed in the patent agent examination. The patent agent exam is conducted by the Indian Patent Office almost every year. Once they have qualified and paid the required fees, their name is included in the register of patent agents. Patent agents are allowed to draft and file a patent application on behalf of others. Often, they are employed either by the Indian government to evaluate pending patent applications, or by patent firms that help companies and individuals to file patents.

A patent attorney can also be a patent agent, if they have passed the exam and qualified as such. A patent agent can be a patent attorney only if they have a law degree and are a member of the bar.

1.5 Patent Drafting Firms in India

Often the patent agents and patent attorneys belong to various IP and patent firms which offer their services for clients who want to file patents in India.

They offer different packages of services for filing in India patent offices or globally including US Patent office and WIPO. They can help in the drafting process for the patent, filing of the patent in the patent offices, keeping track of it until it gets granted, renewal of patents etc.

Examples of such firms include IPMetrix, Foxmandal, Clairvoyate, Banana IP, PatnTech, IntePat, IPFlair etc. Their fees start from around Rs 15000 for India filings and more for international filings, depending on the number and type of services needed. Many corporate houses and IT companies hire such patent firms to draft the patents invented by their employees and researchers.

1.6 Conclusion

In this chapter we have briefly gone through the various types of Intellectual Property and the laws related to patents in India. In the following chapters we shall discuss in more detail about patents specifically.

Chapter 2: Introduction to patents

———

In this chapter we introduce what is a patent and what are the main components of a patent filing.

2.1 What is a patent

A patent is a novel idea of an invention that is documented and filed with a patent body. Examples of patent bodies are India Patent Office, World Intellectual Property Organization WIPO and US Patent Office USPTO.

Patenting an idea gives protection to the invention from others copying and profiting from it. The patent idea usually solves a previously unsolved problem, or solves it in a better or more efficient way compared to existing solutions in that area or domain.

2.2 Criteria for patentability of an idea

In order to be approved, a patent has to pass the patentability criteria such as novelty, non-obviousness, usability etc. In plain English, some of the guidelines are as follows:

• **Novelty**: The idea being patented has to be unique in the world, i.e. nobody else should have published or used the same idea.

• **Non-Obviousness or Inventive Step**: The idea should have some step that is extra and non-trivial improvement over merely a combination of existing techniques. It cannot be simply a combination of existing ideas that other experts in the same area would think as obvious.

• **Utility**: It has to have an actual utility or perform a useful function. This implies that the idea might eventually be capable of developing into a useful product that is used by customers.

• **Detectability**: It should be easy to detect infringement of the idea, if someone has copied it.

• **Feasibility**: It should be feasible to implement the idea using current knowledge and technology. For example, a time machine idea may be novel and non-obvious, even perform a useful function, but it is not feasible to implement using today's technology.

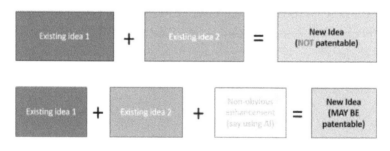

Figure: An illustration of which idea may or may not be patentable, based on non-obviousness criterion.

2.3 Types of patents and other Intellectual Property

As mentioned previously, there are multiple types of intellectual property or IP, such as trademarks, copyrights etc. and patent is just one of them. There are also multiple types of patents such as design patents, standards patents, utility patents etc.

The common types of ideas that software engineers or tech companies might like to patent are:

- **Utility patents**: These present the design of a system or method that performs a utility.
- **Standards patents:** These are more common in a few domains such as the networks domain, where the inventor is proposing a new standard in, say, mobile wireless technology, and could get money out of licensing the patent to third parties.

There are also system patents, that protect the whole product as system comprising of various components, and process patents that protect the process used to manufacture a product. Many pharmaceutical companies inventing new drugs might patent the chemical composition and method of manufacture of the drug.

There are also different types of patent applications including the following:

- **Provisional Specification (PS):** These do not contain claims but only a short description, summary and diagrams related to the patent. These are drafted to secure the earliest date of the patent. These are cheaper to file and are not examined by patent examiners.
- **Complete Specification (CS):** These include the full details of the patent including claims. These are examined by patent examiners and the patent is either

granted or rejected.

- **Patent of Addition**: These are additional claims and additions to an already filed patent application.
- **International Patent Application or PCT Application**: These are patents under the PCT treaty, which allows one to file in any one patent office such as in India and if granted, the patent will be valid in multiple countries.

2.4 Time taken for the granting of a patent

The process of getting a grant for a filed patent takes several years before the patent office, for a patent examiner to examine it, search for prior arts, obtain any clarifications from the inventors and finally approve the grant.

This time can be as low as 2 years and as high as 5 or 6 years in some cases. Many times, patents filed in India patent offices may take a longer time than those filed in the US patent office.

Therefore, if a company states "patent filed" on a product, it does not mean that patent has actually been granted. A significant percentage of filed patents are eventually rejected by the patent offices. However, stating such a thing does give a sense of prestige to the product that it is somehow unique or better than competing products, which is why this is sometimes stated in advertisements for the product.

2.5 Reasons to patent a new idea

Any new and novel idea need not be patented to prove to the world that the inventor got it first: It can also be published as a research paper, technical report or white paper, or made public in a blog post or article. One may choose not to publish the idea anywhere and keep it as a trade secret, so that competitors may never get to know of it in the first place. There is also an avenue called "Defensive Publication" which is not as strong as a patent, but gives some rights for protecting the idea or invention.

The main reason for filing a patent for an idea is the possibility of future monetary benefits to the inventor or the company, along with giving due credit to the inventor for the inventive idea. A patent gives the inventor legal protection from others infringing it, for a fixed period (usually 20 years). In this time, anyone else who wants to use the idea would now have to negotiate with the inventors for a license or for buying the patent from them.

If it is a small company or startup with only one novel idea as the USP (unique selling point), it makes sense to patent it. A patent is a form of property or asset and usually carries a monetary value. It also results in prestige and credibility in the minds of the public (even though it might not always be justified), i.e. a company that has obtained granted patents for its products must be a good company.

Filing a patent can be useful for an inventor or a company to safeguard their inventive idea. It can be used in patent portfolio negotiations between companies, where a group of patents is licensed as a unit. A patent filing may be out of a defensive or offensive motivation. This means, a patent might be filed to keep others from suing the inventors or company (defensive), or it might be filed primarily to sue others and make money out of them (offensive). Patent trolls (individuals or companies) have been known to do exactly such a thing.

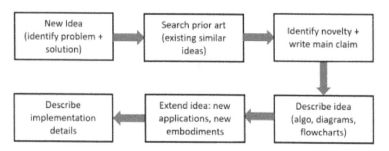

Figure: Steps from an initial idea to a patent document

2.6 Components of a patent application

In order to file, a patent idea needs to have enough information about the following components:

United States Patent [19]

Gilhousen et al.

[11] Patent Number: 4,901,307

[45] Date of Patent: Feb. 13, 1990

[54] SPREAD SPECTRUM MULTIPLE ACCESS COMMUNICATION SYSTEM USING SATELLITE OR TERRESTRIAL REPEATERS

[75] Inventors: Klein S. Gilhousen, San Diego; Irwin M. Jacobs, La Jolla; Lindsay A. Weaver, Jr., San Diego, all of Calif.

[73] Assignee: Qualcomm, Inc., San Diego, Calif.

[21] Appl. No.: 631,265

[22] Filed: Oct. 17, 1990

[51] Int. Cl.⁵ H04J 13/00
[52] U.S. Cl. 370/18; 375/1
[58] Field of Search 370/18, 19, 95; 375/1

[56] References Cited

U.S. PATENT DOCUMENTS

OTHER PUBLICATIONS

IEEE Communications, vol. 24, No. 1, Feb. 1986, pp. 8–15, Cellular System Design: An Emerging Engineering Discipline, James F. Whitehead.

ABSTRACT

A multiple access, spread spectrum communication system and method for providing high capacity communications to, from, or between a plurality of system users, using code-division-spread-spectrum communication signals.

40 Claims, 12 Drawing Sheets

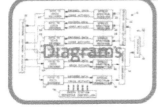

What we claim is: 5
1. A multiple access, spread spectrum communication system, comprising:
  means for communicating information signals between at least two of a plurality of system users using code-division-spread-spectrum communica- 10 tion signals;
  isolation means, coupled to said means for communicating, for unequally weighting signal power of said code-division-spread-spectrum communication signals, wherein said isolation means com- 15 prises:
  activity detectors means for measuring signal activity levels for said information signals relative to a no activity level over a predetermined sampling time and for providing an activity signal corresponding 20 to measured activity; and
  power control means coupled to said means for communicating for adjusting a transmission power duty cycle for said code-division-spread-spectrum communication signals in response to changes in said 25 activity signal.
2. A multiple access, spread spectrum communication system, comprising:

Figure: Important components of a patent

Title: a short line that describes mainly the domain of the patent idea. Typically it does not mention the actual unique claim.

Abstract or short description: This summarizes the patent idea and its unique claim in a few short sentences, typically not exceeding 150 words.

Long description of the invention: This is where the inventor describes the idea, the technical details of its implementation, and the use cases in full detail.

Diagrams/ flowcharts/ illustrations: These are added to the description to give a better idea of how the patent is to be used, how it is implemented, what is the user interface, the system diagram, architecture, flow diagrams.

A list of claims. The claims are the main legal part of the patent, which would be examined to determine whether the patent should be granted or not. This can be either as system based claims or method based claims. There can be independent claims and dependent or derived claims, derived from the independent claims.

The wording of an independent claim might be something like "*System and method for <some function>, comprising <the components of the system or steps of the method>*". A dependent claim may have a wording such as "*System based in claim 1, where <some modification to the independent claim>*".

The basic method of patenting is quite simple: make a document with a description of the idea, add diagrams, flowcharts and technical details of how to achieve or implement the idea. Then write the set of claims. Then file the document, in the requisite format along with details of inventors, with the patent office, along with the patent filing fees. Usually most offices have the option for online filing of patents.

It is better to include as many diagrams, flowcharts and algorithms, equations, illustrations as possible. This gives a better understanding of the idea and helps to convince the patent examiner that the idea is feasible to implement and so should be granted, if it is found novel. Also, it is better to think about the original idea and include multiple use cases of the idea, and multiple ways in which the idea can be extended. This covers the possibility of someone stealing the idea and claiming the different use case is not covered by the patent.

2.7 Are software ideas patentable?

It is indeed more difficult to patent a purely software idea than an idea that is implementable in hardware, or has a mixture of hardware and software components. Part of the reason is that it is difficult to prove that a purely software idea (or 'method') is indeed patentable and is not simply a combination of existing methods.

Also, a pure software algorithm is quite difficult to patent. Someone could simply argue that the software algorithm is derived from research papers or break the algorithm into a number of small steps and claim that each of the small steps is already well known or published.

Besides, if the software based patent candidate idea does not have a front-end (i.e. it runs in the background), it is difficult to prove infringement of it in a court, since someone could claim that they reproduced the same functionality using a different software algorithm. So it is better for a patent to have a front-end or user interface as an integral part of the invention.

The 'system' ideas, which try to patent the whole system of hardware and/or software components, are easier to prove that they are indeed novel. So a system idea is better (and stronger) than a method idea. Similarly, a method idea with a front-end is better than one without a front end.

Also, just because a patent is granted by a patent office does not mean that the inventor or company can actually make money out of it. It should be something that others (competitors) might be tempted to copy in order to get revenue from selling the product that holds the patent idea.

2.8 Cost of filing a patent

The cost of filing a patent varies enormously, from a few thousand rupees (around a couple of hundred dollars) in the India patent office to a few thousand dollars in USPTO or WIPO.

If one engages a patent agent or attorney to file the patent for them, the cost will probably go higher. Alternatively, one can simply read some existing patents, get an idea of the structure and draft one themselves. However, a trained patent attorney might be able to draft a patent in a way that makes it more likely to be granted.

Governments in some countries like India have set up incentives for small companies and inventors, such as lower patent filing costs for startups which meet certain criteria.

2.9 Conclusion

In this chapter, we have discussed different aspects related to patents including patenting criteria and components of a patent.

Chapter 3: Making a stronger patent application: Prior art search, design thinking and TRIZ

———

In this chapter we discuss a few ways in which patents can be made stronger, while drafting a patent. This is mainly from the point of view of the inventors of the patent.

One important step is to conduct a comprehensive patent search using various tools. Another is to expand the original idea using various strategies. Another is to make a prototype of the idea and survey its benefits with the users of the product.

3.1 Tools for conducting a prior art search of an idea

Before drafting a patent, one should make sure the idea is not existing already. This is because drafting a patent needs considerable time and money, one should make sure it is actually worth the effort.

Prior art search is the step where one searches in the literature to make sure the idea being claimed as novel is not already in the public domain.

Figure: Patent prior art search using WIPO Patentscape tool

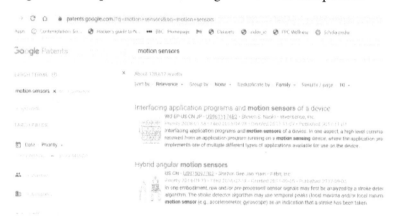

Figure: Patent prior art search using patents.google.com tool

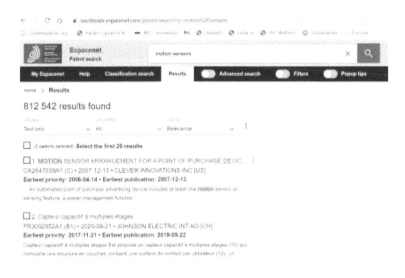

Figure: Patent prior art search using Espacenet tool

Figure: Patent prior art search using lens.org

Figure: India patent office website INPASS for Patent search

Some common patent search tools include the following:

- Google patents https://patents.google.com/ and Google patent search https://www.google.com/?tbm=pts
- WIPO Patentscope https://patentscope.wipo.int/search/en/search.jsf
- USPTO patent search for US patents https://www.uspto.gov/patents/search
- Espacenet patent search for European patents https://www.epo.org/searching-for-patents/technical/espacenet.html
- The Lens https://www.lens.org/
- Clarivate patent search tools https://clarivate.com/

derwent/solutions/derwent-innovation/
- India patent search website INPASS https://ipindiaservices.gov.in/publicsearch

These tools can be useful for conducting a prior art search. One should put in the keywords related to technologies used in the idea and then examine to resulting list of patents returned by the search tool to determine if the existing patent is covering the whole of part of the claimed idea.

Since the idea might already be published in the research domain rather than as a patent, one should also search in academic or research papers, using Google scholar or IEEE Explore or Microsoft academic search or any other academic paper search engine (https://en.wikipedia.org/wiki/ List_of_academic_databases_and_search_engines). One should additionally do a general web search (using a search engine such as Google or Bing).

3.2 Making a patent landscape of the area

An important step while exploring a new area is to make a patent landscape of an area. A patent landscape helps one to get an idea of how much of the area is already covered by existing patents. This can assist in focusing the ideation and development of products, since making a product in what is already patented means one would have to give royalties to the existing patent holders.

The steps for making a patent landscape include the following:

- Make a list of topics and keywords related to the area

• Search patents using a patent tool for these keywords and permutations

• Get the top few patents in each sub-area, say top 5

• Make an excel spreadsheet including the found patents

• Then analyze the found patents: group by company, by topic, by year (to identify emerging topics) etc

• Collect results in a patent landscape report

• On the basis of the report, draw conclusions and learnings about what is already covered, what is not yet covered, emerging areas etc.

In the following sections, we discuss some strategies to make an idea more patentable or stronger.

There are certain strategies that can help a budding inventor to make one's idea more patentable.

The best strategy for complete beginners would be: go to google patents and read some of the existing patents, see how the patent language works. There is a certain amount of legalese there, that one needs to be familiar with.

After that, one can use one of the strategies in the following subsections to make or enhance a patentable idea.

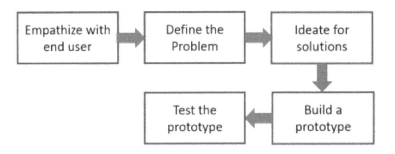

Figure: Approach of design thinking

3.3 Design thinking or user centered thinking.

Design thinking is also called user centered thinking. It means thinking from the point of view of the users and other stakeholders of different ways to solve the problem, not just thinking from the perspective of a product developer or manufacturer. An important quality here is empathy with the user and putting oneself in the user's shoes.

Some of the steps in design thinking are as follows:

• One conducts different kinds of quantitative or qualitative (via questionnaires or interviews) user surveys to get an idea of the actual problems faced by the users from their point of view, so that the solution, in the form of a patent, can be much more comprehensive.

• After this, one makes a quick design prototype of the solution. There are a number of software prototyping tools and apps (such as marvel app, proto.io) available for this purpose.

• After building the prototype, one then conducts user trials to get some idea if the prototype of the invention actually solves the original problem or if there might be other ways of solving the same problem.

3.4 TRIZ (Theory of Inventive Problem Solving)

TRIZ is a strategy which enables one to expand the idea in different directions by systematically examining all permutations of the idea. It was developed by the Soviet scientist Altshuller, who studied 40000 patent abstracts to understand how inventors were patenting their inventions, and used it to generalize strategies which were collected as part of the TRIZ methodology.

TRIZ enables one to expand the original idea in different directions by going from the specific problem to the generalized problem, then to the general solution of all similar problems and back to the specific solution of the problem being considered. An example of its application can be, generalizing a specific problem, trying multiple creative solutions to the problem, then selecting the solution that best fits the specific case.

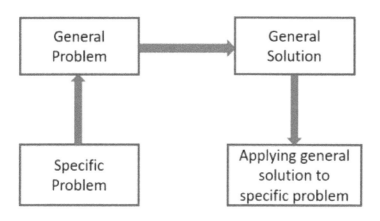

Figure: Approach of TRIZ

Another example can be, breaking a machine into components and then thinking how each component can be replaced so that the overall efficiency of the machine is maintained but the components are cheaper, or that the cost is maintained but the efficiency is increased in some way, or that the machine does an additional function that solves a problem it could not solve before.

To illustrate how TRIZ can be used to determine how to get around or bypass an existing patent in an area, one can ask the following questions related to the idea or solution:

• Divide their solution into smaller parts

• For each part, try to propose an alternative method

• See if any part can be improved with machine learning

• See if the order of the components can be changed or reversed

• See if any parts can be parallelized

• See if some of the functions can be removed, combined or done in advance

• See if the same architecture or part of it can be abstracted out and used for a novel application or using a novel technology

• Can any of the actions be made periodic instead of continuous, or vice versa?

• Can any of the components be replaced by a cheaper or faster component?

Some references on TRIZ are as follows:

• How TRIZ can be applied in the software domain https://triz-journal.com/triz-software-40-principle-analogies-sequel/

• https://en.wikipedia.org/wiki/TRIZ

• A number of websites explain how TRIZ can be applied in the software domain (such as https://triz-journal.com/triz-software-40-principle-analogies-sequel/)

3.5 Extending the idea

One should think creatively about extending the original idea in all possible directions, applying it to all possible use cases, all possible embodiments or ways of applying it, all possible kinds of extensions in different domains, etc. This has the benefit of making the patent stronger, so that any competitor would not be able to bypass it in order to solve a problem and would be forced to pay royalty fees to license it.

3.6 Generalizing the claims of the idea

Another strategy is to generalize the claims as much as possible, so as not to limit the claims to any one specific way of implementation or any one technology.

The language of the claims should be broad enough to even cover any technologies developed in the future, however narrow enough to not cover any existing patents or solutions already in the market.

3.7 Conclusion

In this chapter, we have considered a few ways to make an existing patent stronger, for example by using tools such as design thinking and TRIZ.

Chapter 4: How to file a patent in India

In this chapter we discuss some aspects of patent filing in different patent offices in India.

4.1 Where to file the patent application

As mentioned earlier, patents can be of multiple types. One needs to decide what type of patent to file and where to file it.

For example, a product such as a model of a mobile phone, which is going to be used by customers in multiple countries, will need protection of its unique aspects in all these countries. So one can file a WIPO application under the Patent Cooperation Treaty or PCT. If the product is mainly used in the US market, it is useful to file the patent with USPTO or US Patent Office. To do that, one first needs to apply for foreign filing with the India patent office. If a product is to be used mainly in India, the application can be filed with the Indian patent office.

One may file a provisional patent specification with some basic details to quickly protect the date of the invention, and file a complete specification later.

One may decide to file an entirely new patent for a modification of an existing patented idea, or can file a patent of addition.

4.2 How to file the patent application in India patent office

The first step is to prepare the patent application in the correct format and having all the components such as title, descriptions, list of claims, drawings etc. There are also a few forms for the inventors to sign with their address and other details. There is a form to give the power of attorney to the patent agent, if it is being filed through them. Some of the important forms are as follows:

• **Form 1**: Application for grant of patent, in the specified format with all details.

• **Form 2**: Provisional or complete specification of the patent including field and background and detailed description of the patent, drawings and claims of the patent.

• **Form 3**: Statement and undertaking. This is mainly in the case where the patent has to be filed in foreign countries as well.

• **Form 5**: Declaration of inventorship by the inventors, in case the person filing the application is not the inventor.

• **Form 26**: Power of attorney granted to the patent agent or IP form by the inventors.

The inventors can file the application via registered patent agents or patent firms. They can also file it themselves at the patent office.

A schedule of the fees related to various aspects of Indian patents is available online at the India patent office website. The URL for the same is https://ipindia.gov.in/writereaddata/Portal/ev/schedules/Schedule_1.pdf

Based on the location of the inventor or company, they have to decide which of the India patent offices to submit the application. It can be to the head office in Kolkata or the offices in Mumbai, Delhi or Chennai.

To file a patent, hard copies of the patent application can be sent to the patent office, along with proof of the required fees payment. Alternatively, the filing can be done online. There is a facility for online filing or e-filing available in the India patent office website https://ipindia.gov.in/e-gateways.htm

Figure: India Patent office website for e-filing of patent applications https://ipindiaonline.gov.in/epatentfiling/goForLogin/doLogin

"FORM 1 THE PATENTS ACT 1970 (39 of 1970) and THE PATENTS RULES, 2003 **APPLICATION FOR GRANT OF PATENT** (See section 7, 54 and 135 and sub-rule (1) of rule 20]		(FOR OFFICE USE ONLY)	
	Application No.		
	Filing date:		
	Amount of Fee paid:		
	CBR No:		
	Signature:		
1. APPLICANT'S REFERENCE / IDENTIFICATION NO. (AS ALLOTTED BY OFFICE)			

2. TYPE OF APPLICATION [Please tick (✓) at the appropriate category]

Ordinary ( )		Convention ( )		PCT-NP ( )	
Divisional ( )	Patent of Addition ( )	Divisional ( )	Patent of Addition ( )	Divisional ( )	Patent of Addition ( )

3A. APPLICANT(S)

Name in Full	Nationality	Country of Residence	Address of the Applicant	
			House No.	
			Street	
			City	
			State	
			Country	
			Pin code	

3B. CATEGORY OF APPLICANT [Please tick (✓) at the appropriate category]

Natural Person ( )	Other than Natural Person		
	Small Entity ( )	Startup ( )	Others ( )

Figure: Screenshot of form 1, application for grant of patent, of the patent application at the India Patent Office

FORM 2
THE PATENT ACT 1970
(39 of 1970)
&
The Patents Rules, 2003
PROVISIONAL/COMPLETE SPECIFICATION
(See section 10 and rule13)

1. TITLE OF THE INVENTION

2. APPLICANT (S)
(a) NAME:
(b) NATIONALITY:
(c) ADDRESS:

3. PREAMBLE TO THE DESCRIPTION

PROVISIONAL	COMPLETE
The following specification describes the invention.	The following specification particularly describes the invention and the manner in which it is to be performed.

4. DESCRIPTION (Description shall start from next page.)

5. CLAIMS (not applicable for provisional specification. Claims should start with the preamble — **"I/we claim"** on separate page)

6. DATE AND SIGNATURE (to be given at the end of last page of specification)

7. ABSTRACT OF THE INVENTION (to be given along with complete specification on separate page)

Note: ..

Figure: Screenshot of form 2 of the patent application, comprising provisional or complete specification, at the India Patent Office

FORM 3	
THE PATENTS ACT, 1970	
(39 of 1970)	
and	
THE PATENTS RULES, 2003	
STATEMENT AND UNDERTAKING UNDER SECTION 8	
(See section 8; Rule 12)	

1. Name of the applicant(s).	I/We... .... hereby declare:
2. Name, address and nationality of the joint applicant.	(i) that I/We have not made any application for the same/substantially the same invention outside India Or (ii) that I/We who have made this application No......dated ....alone/jointly with ...., made for the same/ substantially same invention, application(s) for patent in the other countries, the particulars of which are given below:

Name of the country	Date of application	Application on No.	Status of the application	Date of publication	Date of grant

3. Name and address of the assignee	(iii) that the rights in the application(s) has/have been assigned to...

Figure: Screenshot of form 3, statement of undertaking of the patent application at the India Patent Office

F O R M 5
THE PATENTS ACT, 1970
(39 of 1970)

&

The Patents Rules, 2003
DECLARATION AS TO INVENTORSHIP
[See section 10(6) and rule 13(6)]

1. NAME OF APPLICANT (S)

hereby declare that the true and first inventor(s) of the invention disclosed in the complete specification filed in pursuance of my /our application numbered dated is/are

2. INVENTOR (S)
(a) NAME
(b) NATIONALITY
(c) ADDRESS

Dated this .... day of.................. 20............

Signature: -
Name of the signatory: -

3. DECLARATION TO BE GIVEN WHEN THE APPLICATION IN INDIA IS FILED BY THE APPLICANT (S) IN THE CONVENTION COUNTRY: -
We the applicant(s) in the convention country hereby declare that our right to apply for a patent in India is by way of assignment from the true and first inventor(s).

Dated this .... day of.................. 20............

Signature: -
Name of the signatory: -

4. STATEMENT (to be signed by the additional inventor(s) not mentioned in the application form)
I/We assent to the invention referred to in the above declaration, being included in the complete specification filed in pursuance of the stated application.

Dated this .... day of.................. 20............

Signature of the additional inventor(s): -
Name: -

To, The Controller of Patent
    The Patent Office, at ....

Note
*Repeat boxes in case of more than one entry.
*To be signed by the applicant(s) or by authorized registered patent agent otherwise where mentioned.
*Name of the inventor and applicant should be given in full, family name in the beginning .
*Complete address of the inventor should be given stating the postal index no./code, state and country.
*Strike out the column which is/ are not applicable

Figure: Screenshot of form 5, declaration of inventorship of the patent application at the India Patent Office

FIGURE: US PATENT OFFICE (USPTO) website for e-filing of patent applications https://www.uspto.gov/patents/apply

In order to do e-filing for the patent, one needs to have the facility for digitally signing the patent applications. One also needs to furnish details such as their Aadhaar card and payment details.

4.3 Steps after the filing of the patent

The steps after patent filing are as follows:

- **Publication of patent**: After the patent has been filed with all the required forms and documents in the

Indian patent office, it is normally published and searchable after a period of 18 months. For that period, it cannot be searched.

- **Request for Examination**: After this, a Request for Examination or RFE needs to be filed with the India patent office, requesting them to examine the patent and consider the grant.
- **First Examiner Report**: The patent examiners employed at the patent office then issue a first examiner report or FER. The FER report may contain a list of objections as to why the patent application does not satisfy the patentability criteria of novelty and non-obviousness etc. It may also contain existing patents which already include the claimed features.
- **Response to the FER**: The inventors or their agents have to then respond to the objections, after which the patent is again examined. This process may go on for a few iterations.
- **Grant of patent**: After this, the patent may get granted, or rejected and abandoned.
- **Yearly fees**: After the grant, the yearly fees for maintaining the patent have to be paid by the inventors. The normal period of time for a patent is 20 years.

If an inventor has engaged a law firm or patent attorney to handle the paperwork, they will take care of all of these steps and liaise with the patent office. The law firm may charge the inventor or patent owner additional fees per year, additional to the patent filing fees, for this service.

4.4 Checking the filing status of the patent application

Different countries have their own websites for checking the status of a filed patent.

For example, USPTO has PublicPair website where one can check the publicly available information on filed patent applications. It also has a and PrivatePair website for non-public information. The URL is https://www.uspto.gov/patents/apply/checking-application-status/check-filing-status-your-patent-application and https://portal.uspto.gov/pair/PublicPair

Similarly, the inventors can login at the India patent office website and check the status of their patent applications.

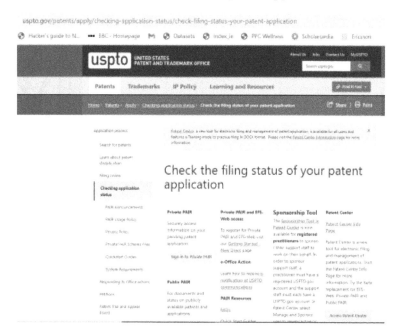

Figure: US Patent office public pair website for checking the status of ongoing patent applications https://portal.uspto.gov/pair/PublicPair

Figure: Screenshot of the USPTO public pair website to check the status of filed patents at https://portal.uspto.gov/pair/PublicPair

4.5 Conclusion

In this chapter, we have considered a few aspects of patent filing at the India patent office and elsewhere.

Chapter 5: Legal process on patent infringement and revocation

———

In this chapter we go through the legal process on how the grant of patents can be opposed by interested parties, including revocation of a patent. We also cover how one can sue another party for patent infringement.

Infringement of a patent is where a product being sold or manufactured copies another product that has been granted a patent earlier, or while making it copies the process of a patented product where the process of its manufacturing has been patented.

Apart from patent infringement, any person can also file a case for declaring an existing granted patent as invalid, by supplying evidence to the court that it does not follow the requirements for a granted patent. This also includes revocation of the patent. For example, they can prove that the patent is not novel or is obvious, or that it was in the public domain earlier than the claimed date of the patent.

5.1 Patent Opposition and Revocation

An existing patent can be opposed by any party. This can take place for various reasons, such as the patent has been wrongly granted. There is a defined process for opposition and revocation. The interested party has to file an opposition application with the controller of patents within six months of the date of publication of the patent (if the opposition is pre-grant or before the patent is granted) or one year from the grant of the patent (if it is post-grant). They have to file the form with all the evidence and other documents.

In India, pre grant opposition can be filed by anyone but post grant can be filed only by interested parties, i.e. parties who will be affected by the grant of the patent, such as those who have a competing product in the same field.

For a post grant opposition application, an opposition board is created by the controller to look at the evidence. There is a hearing with both the parties, after the board submits its report. As a result, the controller may revoke the patent or order it to be amended in the light of the opposition. The decisions of the board can also be appealed with an appellate board, or can be appealed in the courts.

5.2 Patent Infringement

As per the Patents act 1970, the sections 104 onwards discuss the suits concerning infringement of patents.

In any suit for infringement of a patent, where the subject matter of patent is a process for obtaining a product, the court may direct the defendant to prove that the process used by him to obtain the product, identical to the product of the patented process, is different from the patented process if:

(a) the subject matter of the patent is a process for obtaining a new product; or

(b) there is a substantial likelihood that the identical product is made by the process, and the patentee or a person deriving title or interest in the patent from him, has been unable through reasonable efforts to determine the process actually used: Provided that the patentee or a person deriving title or interest in the patent from him first proves that the product is identical to the product directly obtained by the patented process.

5.3 Types of patent infringement

Infringement of an existing granted patent can be of two types:

• **Infringement of a product patent**: An existing granted patent in India can be infringed by a new product that is manufactured or being sold or imported, if the features of the product match the claims of the granted patent.

• **Infringement of a process patent**: Similarly, the process of making a product that has a process related patent, such as manufacturing process of a drug or fertilizer, might be copied.

The claims of the patent are what is protected by patent law.

In case someone in India (or even a foreign entity) suspects that their patent has been infringed by a different product, the following sections mention the steps needed.

5.4 Where a product that might infringe a patent is being imported to India

If the product that is suspected of infringing their patent is from outside India and is being imported, the Intellectual Property Rights (Imported Goods) Enforcement Rules 2007 applied. The person has to file a complaint with the customs authorities with details of the infringement, who will then investigate the complaint and take necessary action.

5.5 Where the product that is suspected of infringement is produced inside India

In this case, the company or individual need to file a petition at an Indian court under the relevant acts such as Patent act, with relevant details, accompanied with a prayer for enforcing their patent rights. The petitioners have to get the certified copies of the patent documents from the India patent office.

The petitioners have to provide proof of how the product is infringing the patent. They also may cite publications and use experts in the field as witnesses to support their arguments.

The court, if it determines that the patent is indeed infringed, can issue an injunction to stop manufacturing the infringing product, as well as damages.

5.6 Court procedure for patent infringement

For a patent infringement case, the normal court procedure takes place, with steps such as arguments, cross examination etc. until the court delivers their judgment and the remedy such as injunction and damages.

Normally, the court cases related to patent infringement are to be filed in the high courts or district courts.

5.7 A few important cases for patent infringement

Information about a few important recent patent infringement cases in Indian high courts and supreme court, such as Novartis vs Cipla (2015) and Bajaj vs TVS (2009) are given in the ipleaders website. URL: https://blog.ipleaders.in/patent-infringement-cases-india/

More information about the order passed in the Novartis vs Cipla (2015) case are given in the Indian Kanoon website URL: https://indiankanoon.org/doc/68879740/

The verdict in the Bajaj Auto vs TVS Motor case (2009) is given here:

URL: https://indiankanoon.org/doc/1058259/

5.8 Conclusion

In this chapter, we have considered a few aspects related to patent opposition and infringement, and the process for the same in India.

Chapter 6: Conclusion

———

In this book, we have gone through the various aspects of patents and patent filing process. We have focused on patents rather than other Ips such as copyright. We have mentioned the steps that are to be taken for ideation, and how to make a better patent.

Generally speaking, patenting is a skill that can be enhanced mainly by practice. As far as the learning to draft a patent is concerned, the best way is to read multiple patents in the same domain and try to understand the idea being patented.

There are both good and bad sides of patenting, and the system is not quite perfect. Some people might argue that patenting actually kills innovation instead of encouraging it, because the larger companies with their army of lawyers have an undue advantage.

However, patenting still gives an inventor a way of monetizing and getting credit for their original idea. Despite its drawbacks, the benefits of patenting are quite worthwhile.

About the authors

———

Siva Prasad Bose is a retired electrical engineer and writer of introductory guides on aspects of law in India. He received his engineering degree from Jadavpur University, Kolkata and has a law degree from Meerut University, Meerut. His interests lie in the fields of family law, civil law, law of contracts, and any areas of law related to power electricity related issues.

Joy Bose is a data scientist and researcher by profession. He has 6 granted patents in USPTO, 2 granted patents in India Patent Office, and more than 20 filed patents in various patent offices.

Other Books by Siva Prasad Bose

Did you love *Introduction to Patents and Patent Law in India*? Then you should read *Self Publish Books and e-Books in India*[1] by Siva Prasad Bose and Joy Bose!

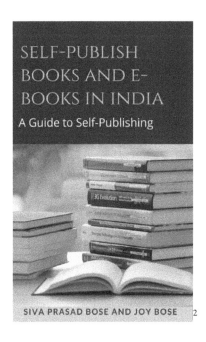

Self-publishing is getting common nowadays due to the low upfront costs for authors and accessibility of digital technologies and web-based publishing software. In countries like India, authors are increasingly using self-publishing tools as they are becoming more widely available in English as well as regional languages. Moreover, the platforms to sell the books that are self-published are also becoming more easily accessible and affordable.

1. https://books2read.com/u/mddD6E

2. https://books2read.com/u/mddD6E

In this book, we discuss the steps for an author to self-publish their manuscript. We go through some of the various tools and platforms currently available and how to use them.

About the Author

Siva Prasad Bose is an electrical engineer by profession. He is currently retired after many years of service in Uttar Pradesh Power Corporation Limited. He received his engineering degree from Jadavpur University, Kolkata and has a law degree from Meerut University, Meerut. His interests lie in the fields of family law, civil law, law of contracts, and any areas of law related to power electricity related issues.

Read more at https://sivaprasadbose.wordpress.com/.

Milton Keynes UK
Ingram Content Group UK Ltd.
UKHW030906160924
448404UK00001B/33